Createspace & Kindle
Self-Publishing Masterclass

OPTIMIZE YOUR BOOK FOR AMAZON

How to Tune-Up Your Kindle
Books for Better Visibility and More
Sales

by

Rick Smith

1

Sell More Books On Amazon Without Spending A Dime...

The Kindle Store is a powerful marketing machine, designed to sell millions of books. There are lots of levers you can pull to make it work better for your book, but most Independent Authors and Self-Publishers don't do anywhere enough *Optimization* to make a difference. Maybe it looks too technical and challenging; but it needn't be.

You've put a lot of effort into writing your book, so adding just one more day to tune-up your *publishing package* is a small investment for a potentially huge reward. This book will show you the systematic way to quickly optimize the five critical factors that will determine whether your book is visible or invisible on Amazon. *If they find you, they will buy you.*

For the first time, the *Top-5 Secret Weapons* to Optimize Your Book for Amazon are integrated into a clear system that everyone can follow. You choose which ones to use right now and work on introducing the others later, or work right through the book and implement all five steps, then watch your book rise in more Amazon search results.

Its an 80/20 process, so if you know which 20% of your effort gets 80% of your results, you can put your energy in the right place and leave yourself plenty of time to get on with writing your next masterpiece. This book will short-cut months of trial and error, and take you straight to the things that *really matter*.

How do the successful Authors and Publishers get their new books noticed? What are the techniques and methods these professionals use every time, to make sure their books show up in more searches, in great positions?

In *Optimize Your Book for Amazon*, Rick Smith lays out a step-by-step plan you can apply to any book...

- Power up your Search Relevance
- Increase your Discoverability
- Create High-Impact Visual Appeal
- Persuade more people to *Look Inside*

...positioning you in the best Amazon Search Results, and making your book visible to many more potential buyers.

The Self-Publishing Masterclass Series

First published in 2013 and now in its Second Edition, *Createspace and Kindle Self-Publishing Masterclass* has sold more than 5000 copies and has more than 100 five-star reviews on amazon.com. This new book, *Optimize Your Book for Amazon*, is part of a series, which also includes *Mile-High Word-Count and Writing Productivity*.

Rick Smith Writes, Collaborates, and Publishes exclusively on Amazon.

Table of Contents

Sell More Books On Amazon Without Spending A Dime... 3

Optimization: How to Do It, And Why You Should 9

Chapter 1 - All About Keywords 19

Chapter 2 - Titles and Subtitles 35

Chapter 3 - Stunning Covers 43

Chapter 4 - Product Description 61

Chapter 5 – Reviews 73

Your Checklist 81

Additional Resources 85

About the Author

Rick Smith is an International Marketing Consultant and Independent Self-Published Author. He writes on an eclectic range of Non-Fiction subjects, including Aviation, Social Science, Technology, Hypnosis, Travel, Health & Fitness, and Writing & Publishing. His many books, including the best-selling *CreateSpace and Kindle Self-Publishing Masterclass,* are consistently in their Category Top-10 lists, and have attracted multiple Best-Seller awards on Amazon.

Rick is also the publisher and author/editor of Young Adult Fiction books by Joey K, and collaborates on Business Books with renowned international Public Speakers such as Michael Jackson and Ryan Hogarth.

7

To check out any of these books, please go to **www.ricksmithbooks.com**

If you're interested in finding out about Rick Smith's *Self-Publishing Masterclass LIVE* events, it's all here at **www.spmasterclass.com**

Optimization: How to Do It, And Why You Should.

If you've written a good book, you owe it to yourself to do everything possible to get it an audience. You've done the hard yards, the bit that most people never ever do; you finished your book. Now you can sit back and wait, and nothing will happen, or you can throw yourself into marketing and promotion, and that doesn't suit everyone's personality.

Optimization is probably the most powerful and least-demanding thing you can do. You won't spend a penny, it's quick and easy, and you'll do everything from your screen, without any social involvement or interaction. It's *passive marketing*, which anyone can do, if they know the right steps.

If you follow the steps in *this* book, you'll make sure that *your* book stands out from the crowd, both in terms of how it performs in Amazon's search engine, and also by persuading more casual shoppers to choose your book for further investigation.

The intention of this book is to provide you with a step-by-step guide so that you can understand why this stuff's important, and how to set it up for your book.

Here are the reasons why you should do it, and the benefits you can expect to receive if you pay some attention to it at the beginning;

To succeed as an Independent Self-Published Author (an *ISPA* from here on), you simply need to be better than the crowd. There's no such thing as a good book or a bad book for the purpose of this exercise. The successful books are those that get search visibility, so unless people go to Amazon looking for a specific title, they are there to browse in a *category* or on a search *keyword*. If your book appears in the Top Row on the screen, it will get more clicks from more people than if it's a few rows down. You must find every possible way to get visibility, by employing a combination of weapons to ensure that when Amazon looks for a book, it finds yours first.

Most ISPA's focus on a very narrow field of view. They know that visibility is critical; so they concentrate on achieving it on one or two search categories, then market to those populations. But the smart guys know that by optimizing well, they can have their books show up in more places, more categories, and more keyword searches. The more places you show up, the more people will ultimately buy your book. It's the digital equivalent of having *widespread distribution.*

It's estimated that well over two million people have written and published at least one book since on-line self-publishing became easily accessible around 2010. Since then, publishing platforms such as Amazon's

Kindle Direct Publishing (KDP) have evolved beyond recognition, and it's never been easier to get your work up in the myriad of online bookstores.

And, if you write a good book and find a way to gain some early sales momentum, you could end up making some pocket money or even a full-time living, if you write a few more books.

How People Shop

Think about how you shop for stuff, especially if you're browsing in a shopping center. You're first drawn towards a collection of items which takes your interest or which are relevant to what you went out to buy. When you look at the collection, your eye is picking out attractive colors and clear text, but at the same time it's looking at the size of the items, perhaps if they're large packages how difficult it will be to get them home, and of course the price is also being compared. You do all this without thinking, and unless you're shopping for an unfamiliar item for the very first time, you quickly make a bunch of calculations and arrive at the decision about which one you're going to buy, or you *disengage*, walk away and look for something different. You're constantly refining your search, by making decisions about where to look, how to choose a shortlist, and what combination of accessibility, price, and presentation will tip you over and make you buy something. That's how you shop in real life.

So when you shop online, particularly when you browse for a book, you may think you're in control of your decision about which one to buy, but there are dozens of nuanced factors being processed in your brain, to enable you to commit to the next stage of the *funnel* as you pass through search screens, sales pages, product descriptions, and *Look Inside*. Added to that, the machinery has already filtered-out thousands of less relevant titles based on your search criteria. It's the same as shopping in real life, you collect and collate, and then you make your decision.

It's this behavior that we harness with *Optimization*; firstly in terms of how we make our book attractive to the Search Engine, which deals with taking the customer to the right section of the store, and secondly to ensure that we optimize every book so that it appeals to the human part of the algorithm, which is all about first impressions.

So, there are things happening *in view*, working on the eyes and in the brains of our potential customers and readers, and there are things happening *out of view*, in the complex digital mechanics of the Amazon platform, and how it tries to short-cut the human decision-making process.

Making money is your objective, but be aware that it can take time. The equation is simple: if you sell some books, you'll receive some royalties. If you don't, you won't. Compared to the amount of work you put in to writing your book, the investment of an extra day or two, polishing the *package* to make it easier for people to discover, is a small input for a major improvement in output. If they can find you, they will buy you.

The intention is definitely *not* to give you tools to game the system. If you want to delve deeply into ninja tricks, there are plenty of them for sale online.

The objective is to show you tools to operate the machine, as it has been designed to operate best. You can bet the big successful publishers and the best independent self-publishers are using all these methods as a matter of course, whenever they publish a book on Amazon. This is the professional way to set up your book.

What is Optimization?

If you understand how the Internet works, in particular how to search for information, then you'll be bumping into SEO (Search Engine Optimization) every day of your life. It's the toolkit that web experts use to tune-up a website so that it rises up the Google Rankings.

Amazon works in the same fundamental way as Google. Amazon is a search engine, and as such it is designed to respond best to optimized books (or any other product it sells) and put them nearer the top of the pile. The more precise the instructions in the product optimization (SEO), the better the engine works on your behalf.

You can view it like a ranking system all of its own. A perfectly optimized book will score 100, where one that has no optimization at all will be at the bottom with zero. All other things being equal, that is how they would appear in the Search Screen, so the optimized book will sell many more than the one at the bottom.

Most ISPA's don't bother with this. They come to the end of the writing process, and maybe they're either fulfilled, or they're simply scared of the 'M' word (marketing) so they never get over that line, and consequently they never make it.

But if you follow the system laid out in this book, it's a relatively simple process that can be done in less than a day, and one which will continue to work for months or years with little or no maintenance.

Why Just Amazon?

The advice in this book, whilst it would largely work across all the major e-book publishing platforms, is specifically targeted at Amazon. Since I began in this business, I have strictly employed Pareto's 80/20 rule, so I have deliberately remained exclusive with Amazon. Here are my reasons:

The Big Dog: Amazon's Market Dominance

Amazon sells around two out of every three e-books worldwide. For ISPA's (that's us) they have ensured that the publishing platform is very easy to use and maintain, compared to others like iBooks and Smashwords.

This unparalleled website and marketing machinery destroys much of the competition, in terms of the flexibility and the opportunities it offers to ISPA's to compete on a level playing field with the big publishers and their blockbuster authors.

Customers love the Amazon website, and Amazon continually invests in keeping it fresh and new, and ever easier to buy what you want with the least number of clicks.

As many people discover for themselves, Amazon's Kindle IOS apps for iPhone and iPad, which constitute a massive part of it's customer base, will only allow you to browse e-books. If you want to actually buy the book, you have to log into your Amazon account using a browser. This is because Apple charges a high royalty on *in-app purchases,* so to avoid them Amazon has to get you out of the Apple walled-garden and onto their own website. This means that the whole storefront experience is played out on every device.

Whilst this introduces the risk of distraction, it's balanced out by the terrific control you have over the way your book is presented on its Sales Page.

Easy to Deal With

When you publish with them, Amazon becomes your Distributor, Reseller, and Customer. Most of this symbiotic relationship is handled automatically, through the KDP dashboard. Amazon reports sales promptly, with plenty of smart online tools you can use to analyze and adjust your book in real time. This enables you, as a one-man (or woman) band, to harness the power of a huge marketing machine, and pull the levers for yourself.

Amazon pays on the nail, too. Sure, you have to wait 60 days for your monthly royalty to arrive, but you know that going in, so you can budget ahead for your business.

And if you have an issue, a simple e-mail to Customer Services will usually get you what you need within 24 hours. Amazon is a pleasure to work with, if you play by their rules.

Why Optimization?

You'll hear the term 'passive income' used a lot in self-publishing circles. The idea is that you write your book then sit back and count your royalties, without having much more to do. This is unlikely even for big name authors on huge publishing deals. They still have to hustle, do chat shows, radio interviews, personal appearances and book signings. That's all marketing, and its all designed to sell more books.

Coming back to earth, it's true that you could have a couple of well-performing books which might pay the bills, but they'll only perform like that if you firstly get them into a strong and visible position, and secondly make sure that they stay there. By using optimization you can achieve both these effects, and it might fairly be called *passive marketing* because you'll have put elements in place that repeatedly trigger in search engines, and keep putting your product in the sight-line of more people who may be willing to buy.

The Twin Effects

Getting Early Visibility

The hottest time for your book is during the first 72 hours after you publish. During this brief period, the Amazon machine is crawling all over your book, looking for signs of life. Any kind of momentum, however small, can start the juices flowing. A rapid rise from (say) Page 5 to Page 3 will shine a light on your book, and if there are other key indicators appearing, such as some sales volume and review activity, it all adds to the impetus.

Maintaining Long-Term Search Position

Once you start to approach a good position, the focus shifts to maintaining your buoyancy. Your optimization now goes into overdrive, because once you're at the top of your search, there'll be a lot more clicks happening around your sales page, and your book will need to sell at least a few copies each day or week to stay up there, even with effective optimization. The Amazon engine has lots of clever ways of sniffing out the winners, so your job is to make sure that you tick as many boxes as possible so that you'll continue to be noticed, and promoted from within.

It Costs Nothing

Optimization costs nothing, apart from some investment of your time and intelligence. Once you understand the five basic items that need to be tuned, you'll simply work through them each time you publish.

- Keywords
- Title
- Cover
- Product Description
- Reviews

By doing it right every time, you'll know that each book you publish has been given the strongest chance of succeeding, and that you haven't left anything out.

External promotions will be more effective and powerful because you know how to leverage the tools, and the optimization multiplies their effectiveness.

Once it's done, apart from occasional tweaks, you can usually forget about it once you have your position. So, lets get started. You can read each section in order, or cherry-pick the subjects that interest you.

Chapter 1 - All About Keywords

What is a Keyword?

A keyword, in the context of internet search, is a particular word or phrase that describes the contents or elements of a Web page. Keywords are intended to act as shortcuts that sum up an entire page. Keywords form part of a Web page's metadata and help search engines match a page to with an appropriate search query.

The importance of keywords is that they are used as an rank-indication of *relevance,* which is one of the most important factors in presenting the right results for each search.

How important is part of the dark art of the big Internet search companies, like Google, YouTube, and Amazon. The effect of keywords in Amazon's search engine is simple to test and track, once you have a bunch of top-selling books in play. But until you do, just be aware that they are important, and learn to work with them.

How Keywords Work

Let's just remind ourselves of the central purpose of Optimizing your book; to equip it all the important hooks so that it will show up in the best possible position in as many searches as possible.

Keywords are the fundamental underpinnings of Optimization. They're the main identifying signs that

—

your *presence*, whether it's a website, a book, a movie, or a blog, is relevant to what somebody's searching for. Keywords are not the *only* factor, but in terms of search visibility they are a very *important* factor that you can control. There are multiple opportunities to place keywords in your Amazon *package* so that they add *relevance* to your book.

The reason why the Keywords section is at the beginning of this book is because getting the keywords right, early in your project, means you start using automatic good habits. This saves you an immense amount of time and frustration later on, for example when you have to find ways to revive a dead book that you didn't prepare properly in the first place.

Some of the IM (Internet Marketing) Gurus will try to convince you that keywords are no longer effective, whilst at the same time trying to sell you their expensive training, or software that gives you some secret sauce to replace keywords. Buyer beware!

Of course there's always more competition, and people got smarter, but that's all the more reason to learn and master optimization, because the well-optimized books rise to the top and stay there, and the rest sink to the bottom. There are millions of well-written but poorly optimized books that prop up the big sellers. Sure, marketing and promotion also play a large part in the life of a successful book, but without solid optimization, even promotions won't work as well, and most books will never gain traction.

In the absence of a demonstrable alternative, keywords remain mighty powerful, and if you can master their use you can dramatically increase the performance of your book on the Amazon store.

When it comes to books, Hope is not a strategy, and Luck needs to be actively found.

Keywords in Search – Priorities

In terms of how books display in a search for a particular 'target' keyword, it's based on an unknown and ever-changing formula, usually referred to as *the algorithm*. Think of it as a math formula that collects all the optimization touch-points of a book on the store, and rates each item according to their position in the *package (manuscript, cover, metadata, and Sales Page)*. In terms of *Relevance*, the basis for the search in play, keywords are the primary selection criteria.

But not all keywords are created equal, and where you place them is equally as important as the words themselves. Most of the tests that have been performed point to the same thing; there is a scale of importance for keywords, depending on where you use them.

So you should always try to use your strongest keywords in the most influential places, which are in order of priority:

Title

Try to get your strongest keyword into your title. Books with their target keyword in their title largely dominate the top rows of viable search categories, almost irrespective of their sales or review performance. There will always be one search term that you *feel* the closest connection with, and which *tests* well for traffic and competition. Putting this keyword (phrase) in your main title is the most important placement. If you do nothing else, this should be your priority. Of course, this is almost exclusive to non-fiction; Fiction is a wholly different story, and not really the subject of this section.

Look at the title of *this* book, and you'll see various keyword combinations are in there, but the most important one is *Self-Publishing.*

Subtitle

Slightly less influential, but definitely a must-have if you can't get good keywords in your main title, is your Sub-Title. If you managed to get your strongest keyword or phrase into your main Title, have a strong secondary word or phrase, and use it here. If you're clever, you can get multiple additional strong keyword combinations into a sub-title, to give you a double-dip effect.

Metadata

These are the seven keywords (five for Createspace), which you're encouraged to enter when you're completing the KDP publishing process. Apparently (allegedly) you shouldn't repeat keywords that are already in your title. In any case, since we know that the

---

Title keywords are most important and are automatically given high priority by the search engine, it's a waste to repeat them in the metadata.

Product Description

Keywords in your Product Description are important too. Search engines and web crawlers look all over a webpage for instances of keywords to index. Your product description is a good place to insert *long-tail* keywords, which may not be searched often, but which will also have very limited competition.

If you can't think of any for yourself, use the Amazon search box. Type in one of your less prominent keywords, and see what Amazon suggests as recent and popular searches. Look towards the bottom of the list and pick out any keywords or phrases that look natural but relatively unpopular. Simply knowing that they have been searched is a reasonable indicator that they will be searched again, and if yours is one of very few books with that key phrase, even if it's only in your product description a couple of times, it could give it boost in the search results. You might then show up somewhere that you hadn't planned, and it adds to the chances of you making a sale.

Look Inside Section

We know that Amazon indexes the entire text of your book, and I categorically proved it in my book "Createspace and Kindle Self-Publishing Masterclass". We also know that Amazon scans and extracts the first

10% of your manuscript, and reformats it for the *Look Inside* section. So it's also reasonable to speculate that keyword occurrences in the first 10% may be more impactful than those further in the book.

But, probably more importantly, if you cleverly sprinkle the optimum keyword density in your Look Inside, they act as a focus and point of reference to anyone who has arrived by searching on that or those particular keywords, acting as a further convincer that your book is relevant, and focused on the very subject they are searching for. That's one of the human factors of optimization.

How to Leverage Keywords

Once you have an optimum set of keywords in your Title and Subtitle, Metadata, Product Description and Text, you are well equipped to trigger the maximum number of search combinations, and show up in the maximum number of places. More visibility will naturally lead to more sales, if your book and its *package* are of acceptable quality.

However, there are some simple things that you can do to utilize and leverage your strongest keywords to gain position and visibility for your book.

Keyword-Buys Increase Relevance

Amazon is always looking for positive reasons to promote your book. If it's selling a few copies a day or a week, and displaying some popularity when compared to other books in its vicinity, the more people that buy the book after searching on your keyword, the higher your book should rank for that keyword. If you can capture the strongest keyword (*e.g. Self-Publishing*) and drive people to use it to search for your book, each successful sale will contribute to Amazon's view of your book's Relevance.

So, relevance is key. It dictates (contributes strongly) to your position in a search on any keywords that you are indexed for. By the way, it doesn't work (noticeably) if you put your keywords in a search URL then distribute the link. This may be because it simply doesn't work, or alternately because a book searched for by keyword which subsequently *isn't* bought may partially or wholly cancel out ones that are bought. Ergo it's a risky strategy. If you distribute a link like this you expect to get many more clicks than buys.

So you need to train people to use *keyword buys*.

This can massively move a book, especially ten or twenty buys in a short space of time, which adds to the Popularity part of the equation.

How to format a Keyword Buy request

When you're online and promoting your book, you'll be hustling in (for example) Facebook Groups for people to download and review your book. When you contact someone using Facebook Messenger (the way these things usually work), you can include wording like this:

Thanks for agreeing to buy/review my book. Please use the following method in the Kindle Store (it helps my rankings)

Search for keyword: **self-publishing**

Position on amazon .com: #47

Position on amazon.co.uk: #26

There's a great Facebook Group at *Fab Friday 99c Promotion Group for Authors* where all the members understand keyword buys.

Once you get to a first page position, you can start giving people a link with the keyword search so it opens a search page with your book visible. Since the URL is the same as if they had manually entered the keyword search, once they click and buy your book, you should be getting the same full benefit of adding a little bit to your relevance score.

You can get a URL for your search by doing it yourself, then copying the long URL from the Browser address box at the top of you screen.

Choosing Keywords

Here's my theory about keywords; you can treat them like a precise science and run endless comparisons until you hit the scientifically perfect and proven combination. Applying Pareto's rule once more, the first 20% of your efforts will give you 80% of your final result. If you keep going, the final 80% of your effort will only give you the final 20% of *total optimization.* Who has the time?

The intention of this book is to give you a quick and simple checklist to run on each book you publish, executed in less than a day so you can get on with writing your next book, or throwing yourself into marketing.

So here are the basics about how to choose a good (but not necessarily perfect) set of keywords for your book's *package.*

Your objective is to build a short-list of ten words or phrases that meet both the following criteria:

- The keyword attracts good search traffic, and
- There is moderate or limited competition for the keyword

The Keyword Attracts Good Search Traffic

When you're thinking about niches and titles, trying to come up with an idea for your next book, search for niches where the subject works as a title and a strong keyword, such as *self-publishing* or *self-hypnosis.*

Here are the tools you can use to build your keyword shortlist. But don't surrender totally to the system; you will *feel* some keywords more than others, so mix your instinct with the science to make choices that feel right and test well.

Amazon's Search

Keywords like *stress* or *meditation* are too broad, and there will be way too many books with those words somewhere in their package. You need a method of choosing *derivatives* of the main keyword, which still have decent traffic, but don't attract so many books.

Use your primary subject keyword, and type it into the search box (set it up for *Kindle Store* and/or *Books* first, because you're not interested in other products). As you type in the phrase, you'll see Amazon start to make suggestions in a drop-down list.

Here's our example for *stress:*

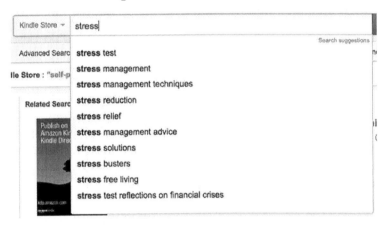

Some experts refer to these as Amazon's 'Leading Indicators' and there is a whole science devoted to interpreting them. For this training, I'll keep it simple. Go slowly, and see how these phrases change as you type more of your phrase, and Amazon auto-fills the list. This is showing you popular and recent searches that have been used by people looking for books in your subject category. This way, you can get a good idea of keywords you might use which you now know are in regular use. In terms of how these keyword phrases are ranked, let's assume that *popularity* and *frequency* are the predominant factors. The higher up the list, the more popular the search.

In a relatively narrow niche, this simple method may be enough to give you a nice list. Think laterally, and explore related key phrases. You might discover something you hadn't thought of. Each time a search screen comes up, you can see the number of results on the top left. Interpreting these is also simple; if you see more than 5000 results for a keyword, that keyword is probably too competitive and you'll struggle to get to the top. If you're seeing results less than 500, you might be looking at a huge opportunity if you have good reasons to believe that the keyword is well searched. Usually, you'll be somewhere in between.

There's some excellent software around if you want to do more scientific comparisons. These work by quickly cataloging the key elements of each book that triggers a particular keyword, and present you with a full analysis of every book, showing price, estimated earnings, sales rank, review scores, and keyword densities. You could do this manually, and it would take days. But using these packages, it happens in a few minutes. This will tell you whether any particular keyword has value.

—

Either is very useful, and both together are even better. Check out the video demo on each website.

AK Elite, **www.akelite.com**

AK Elite is the 'Daddy' of keyword analysis tools, which handles multiple simultaneous keywords, allows you to filter the results on numerous different criteria, and gives a full analysis of reviews. It's not cheap, coming in at $147, however if you're going into the self-publishing business seriously, it will save you hours of research and weeks of trial and error.

Kindle Spy, **www.kdspy com**

Kindle Spy is newer, and runs inside the Amazon page on your browser. It analyzes search pages one at a time, and gives you an instant 'reverse-engineered' picture of what's going on with all the books that are displaying high up. One brilliant feature is that KDSpy will create a *Word Cloud* based on all the book titles, which gives you a great shortlist of keywords that are working well in that group. At $27, I absolutely recommend you get KDSpy and start using it immediately. Right now, it only runs on a Chrome browser, but that's free to download.

By the way, I'm not affiliated to either of these companies. I just like their stuff. It saves time and makes money.

Google Keyword Tool

It's impossible to get an absolute value on the popularity of search keywords (their *traffic*) in Amazon. But you can get a pretty good idea of the *relative* popularity of various keyword combinations.

Not too long ago, there was a free tool on the Internet called the 'Google Keyword Tool'. Google being Google probably figured out that people were using this for activities and research that wasn't earning Google any money (such as choosing keywords for an Amazon book), so suddenly in the summer of 2013, the Keyword Tool disappeared, and millions of Amazon authors and assorted internet freeloaders went into temporary mourning. However, it hadn't actually disappeared, but instead had been folded inside the *Google Adwords* environment.

In fact, the tool is even more sophisticated now. It allows you to type in a prospective search keyword or phrase, and it will then show you the actual numbers of searches performed on that keyword, which you can sort by numerous criteria such as region, country and so on. It will also show you the figures for related searches. If you use this tool, you can then pick the top five or six by volume, or you can look for more precise terms which are less popular, which may be more relevant to your book but against which you will suffer less competition, which will also help your rankings when you use these terms in Amazon. Remember, these are Google's numbers, so you have to be realistic, but it's reasonable to assume that the split of popularity won't be too different from what going on over the road in Amazon's search engine. And as you'll see in a moment, Google Search can be a really serious part of your keyword strategy too.

The Keyword Planner Tool is a feature-packed device, which is too much to explain in detail here, so go and explore it for yourself in Google Adwords. You'll need to open an Adwords account to get access, but you can do that for free and there's no obligation to actually spend any money once you're in there. Just start by Googling 'Adwords', then practice using the tool until you find the way it works best for you.

Google Search

By the way, if you get it right, your use of keywords in Amazon titles can give your book a massive leg-up on Google itself. One of Google's primary criteria for ranking a search result is *Authority*. If you've ever explored Search Engine Optimization (SEO – A dark art practiced by geeks in caves) you'll have heard about Authority. If you have a small business website, you can spend thousands on trying to get up to the front page on Google, but if you don't get Authority into your formula, you'll struggle against bigger competitors.

Well, guess who's the biggest Authority site around? That's right, our good friends Amazon. So if you have a fairly non-competitive keyword phrase in your book title on Amazon, when someone performs that search on Google, it's quite likely that your Title (accompanied by a link to Amazon) will pop up on Page One. Try the old chestnut *'Learning Masonic Ritual'* again. This is the number one search term keyword for the subject, and my book has it as its main title. Last time I looked, it came up as number three worldwide on Google, and I'm absolutely certain that it's adding to my sales as people click straight through from Google to my Amazon Sales Page. Sure, it's a niche book (which consistently sells hundreds of copies every month), but aren't all non-fiction and self-help titles in a niche of some kind?

Keywords Summary

That's enough about keywords for now. Try those two methods, and if you feel the need to go further (the 80% effort for 20% reward) you can. Check the Recommended Reading section at the end of the book.

If you have managed to build your ten-word shortlist, put it to one side. The next few sections will explain how to use each keyword in the right place for maximum effect.

Chapter One Summary

- Keywords are the most important factors in how your book is discovered with Amazon Search.
- Your strongest keyword should form part of your main Title.

- Use your Sub-Title to insert a keyword phrase or phrases.
- Research seven diverse metadata keywords to give you exposure in multiple search groups and niches.
- Insert long-tail keyword phrases in your Product Description, ensuring they work properly in the general language.
- Ask people to use *keyword-buys* when you are promoting your book.
- Make a short-list of ten keywords as your *main set*.
- Choose keywords that *test* well but also *feel* right.
- Use Amazon's Search *Leading Indicators* to pick good niche keywords with less competition.
- Use Google Adwords' *Keyword Planner Tool* to get related keyword ideas and check relative popularity.
- Stick to the 80/20 rule. The first 20% of your effort will get you 80% of your results.

Chapter 2 - Titles and Subtitles

Choosing a Title

Fiction

When it comes to *Title Relevance*, fiction writers are at a serious disadvantage versus non-fiction.

The truth is that your title is not going to help much in Search, so you have to look for other ways to get your novel into the line of vision for people searching in your genre. So for your novel, what's most important in the short term is to design a fabulous cover, and give it a title which will provoke some kind of emotional response when it appears on screen, however it got there.

If you take a look at Kindle's Top-100, both Paid and Free, you'll see numerous examples of titles and covers that convey a *look and feel* to the potential buyer, and that's why they're in the Top 100. It's estimated that around a quarter of titles in the Paid-100 category are new, previously unpublished, or self-published authors, which when you consider that all these books are up against the megastar offerings of the Big-5 Publishers, is pretty good odds.

If you want to see a perfect example of a fiction title that evokes a strong emotional draw, with a cover to match, Gillian Flynn's "Gone Girl" has it all. Even if you're not that interested in the genre (which is left deliberately vague) you almost have to read more. It has sinister undertones, a defined but anonymous victim, it's punchy and edgy, and the simple black cover art really tells you this is a dark, potentially disturbing thriller; exactly the target readership the publisher is seeking.

But nobody is going to go searching for "Gone Girl" in the Amazon search (unless they already saw the advertisements or had the book recommended). The intention here is to illustrate how your imaginative approach to titling and cover design can really tug on the emotions of a potential reader once they have arrived at a place where your book is presented as one of their options.

Genre fiction keywords are massively competitive, because the keyword is the often the genre: *Crime, Romance, Thriller*. Some people looking for fiction will go in through the 'Categories' entrance, and refine their search accordingly until they see the category best sellers. Others will chase authors, either those they've read before or have been recommended to them. As I said at the beginning, my expertise is mainly in non-fiction, so that's where we'll focus next.

Non-Fiction

Choosing Non-Fiction titles is much more scientific, now that you understand the role of *Relevance* in the Search Engine mechanism of Amazon.

Your Non-Fiction Title needs to do three jobs:

- First it must describe clearly what the book is about.
- Secondly, it must contain the primary search terms that people are going to use when they go looking for a book on that subject, and
- Third, it must read well and quickly when people scan the page of search results, so as to draw the eye and get them to dwell on your information.

Your primary objective, once your book cover appears in a search, is to get people to click on it to learn more. Sorry, but they won't come back later, so you get one shot. Your title and cover must work together and draw people in, so spending time (and even some money) on getting this right is, after the quality for your content, the single most important thing about the process.

How Search Works

So let's rewind a little and take a closer look at how the search process works.

Most non-fiction Kindle Books are about how to improve your life in some way or another, or solve a problem, which might range from changing a dripping tap-washer to colonizing Mars. As we said earlier, people generally know what they're looking for, and they'll normally enter something relevant into the search box, because nobody wants to waste time sifting through thousands of vague results. You'll see a lot of *How to, Learning, Beginners Guide To,* and so on.

The Importance of Keywords

If you have a book about Self-Hypnosis, clearly the most important keyword is *Self-Hypnosis,* because even a moron can figure out that anyone looking for a book on Self-Hypnosis is going to start with that as the basis of their search. So, 'Self-Hypnosis' needs to be front-and-center in the Title, and on the Cover Art. And, by the way, so does Self Hypnosis (without the hyphen) because Amazon treats each version as a different Keyword!

Your Title

What the tests show is that, all things being equal, the Keyword in your title outweighs other keyword incidences, so it simply has to be there, for safety. Anecdotally, the ideal place for your keyword is right at the beginning of your title. This will also ensure that, if it is regularly searched, your exact title may start to show up in the drop down list of *Leading Indicators.*

Your Subtitle

Of course people may arrive at your book with keywords that are not your number one. In our Self Hypnosis example, similar keywords such as

---

Hypnotism, Hypnotize, Hypnotic etc. will put your book in the Search Results, but they will rank lower, because they are broader (the key here is in 'Hypno'), and they won't get you up to the top if people are searching for 'Self Hypnosis'.

However, someone searching on one of these keywords will hit your book if it's one of your seven *metadata* keywords. You can also use variants of your keywords in your Subtitle, which is weighted highly as well. Expert opinion these days is that the Subtitle is less relevant than the Main Title, but higher than the metadata keywords. These keywords will work well in a less competitive field, so if you choose well, your book will show up well in some smaller search results.

There are two other important places where keywords feature, one which is well known, and another which is sometimes regarded as an urban legend, although the circumstantial evidence tends to support the conspiracy theorists. First is in your book's Product Description on its Sales Page, sometimes called your 'Blurb', and we'll look at how to write a good Product Description later.

Secondly, keywords in your actual text will affect how your book is found, often in some bizarre and unrelated categories. But since the objective is to show up in more searches, it all adds to the power of your package. If you've read my book *Self-Publishing Masterclass*, there's a demonstration of this, which categorically proves that keywords inside your book are also indexed, and can contribute to you showing up in even more search results.

What is clear is that once you put your book up on Amazon, it searches on your Title, Subtitle, and Keywords, and in your Product Description, during the process of indexing your book in the Search Engine. Conventional wisdom is that you should mention your main keywords around three or four times each in your Product Description, in naturally occurring grammatical language, and this will also help with your relevance in a particular search.

In all these aspects, you're looking to tune-up little one-percent advantages in order to rise up the rankings, so even if this is a tiny factor, you should not ignore it. It may turn out to be more important than you think.

When you browse the non-fiction sections of Amazon, which you should be doing as part of your competitive research, you'll see some quite snappy titles, and some really cumbersome ones too. In the past you might have thought how clumsy they look, but now you should understand that the author is simply trying to cram as many extra keywords (because he's limited to seven elsewhere) into the subtitle, to help with his search rankings. You should be thinking this way too, because your Search Ranking is the single biggest factor in determining the sales success of your book.

Chapter Two Summary

- When choosing a title:
    - Make sure it describes the book, and/or
    - Contains your strongest keyword
    - That the important part is short and snappy and can be read in a thumbnail view
- Pack your Subtitle with keywords and phrases, but make sure it still reads naturally.
- Sprinkle more keywords and phrases through your product description.

Chapter 3 - Stunning Covers

Successful long-term book selling on Amazon depends on its performance in the days and weeks following its launch. The route-one objective is to do whatever is necessary to boost your book in Search Results. If people can see you, you need to entice them to look more closely. This happens in three ways:

1. The visual impact and 'Attraction Factor' of your Cover.

2. The way that your title 'Speaks' to potential customers.

3. The quality of your Product Description.

Once you can persuade Amazon's browsing customer to click on *Look Inside,* the quality of your content takes over.

Smart Indie Authors (and all successful Publishers) put a lot of effort into their covers. Unfortunately, some other people clearly don't get it, or they don't have the confidence to engage with the visual appearance of their product. Many great books never reach their full potential because the cover didn't cut it, and people just went right past. Don't let that happen to you!

So, you might say, *"What does your cover have to do with optimising your book?"* Remember, we said that optimization isn't only about making the best use of Amazon's search engine; it's also about optimizing your

---

book to get real humans to choose it, or at least short-list it for consideration.

The Amazon Search page is a shop window with unlimited display-space. It presents all books equally (apart from position, which is earned), and makes it easy to look at many books in a short space of time. Which is exactly why your cover is so critically important. When people scroll down a page of sixty covers, they're looking for something that grabs their attention, at the very superficial level of image and colour in the first place, and a snappy, readable, relevant title second. If you get those two things right, there's a high probability that they'll click on your cover and go to your Sales Page. Once you have them there, it's yours to lose. If your thumbnail-sized cover lives up to their expectation in the larger format, they may go right to 'Look Inside', and if your writing delivers in the first few paragraphs, you'll sell a book.

Alternately, if they head down to the Product Description, you'll have a great chance to entice them in with your 'blurb'.

But none of this happens if they don't click on your cover. Twice, in fact. People shop with their eyes.

The Keys to Successful Covers

- Covers must be 'Genre-Appropriate'. Book selling has a long history, and there are customs to be observed. Shoppers expect a certain landscape when they search in a genre, and shocking the eye will not usually work.

- Colours must be highly inviting, but also blend into the landscape. If all the competitors' books are blue, choose the most alluring blue you can find and work the magic with your type.

- Titles must be readable in Thumbnail view. Wacky fonts rarely work. You can be both traditional and contemporary. Type choice is both an art and a science, but it's not hard to learn if you figure out what the winners are doing and emulate them.

If you get your cover right, you'll have levelled the field against even the bestsellers. You need to look like a million dollars if you want to get a share of their lunch.

Here are four covers from books in the 'Stress' non-fiction category. See if you can spot the odd one out?

I have read all of these (for research purposes) and I quite liked the red one. For your information, it is currently the lowest ranked of all of them, despite

this is in a
b+w
book!

number two and number four being more than three times its price. Based only on these covers, you'd guess that number one is the best-seller, and it is.

The reason I used these examples is because, apart from the obvious colour and mood discrepancy, the scary title, which would work on a news bulletin or a Men's Health magazine cover, doesn't motivate a book buyer. The other three books paint a picture of calm and tranquillity, with positivity and hope implicit. Our study book is employing a different sales tactic, which is Fear. But most people don't want to hear reinforcement of the shit they're in. They want a quick fix, and that's what the other covers offer.

This is a simple example if the first rule of cover optimization; *give your audience what they expect.* Number one uses the 'customary' palette for this category, which is white, pastel green and blue, but also uses highly effective type styling to stand out from the crowd.

Of course this isn't conclusive proof of anything, but it does reinforce the importance of your cover presentation in driving more customers to 'Look Inside'.

Amazon's Sales Funnel

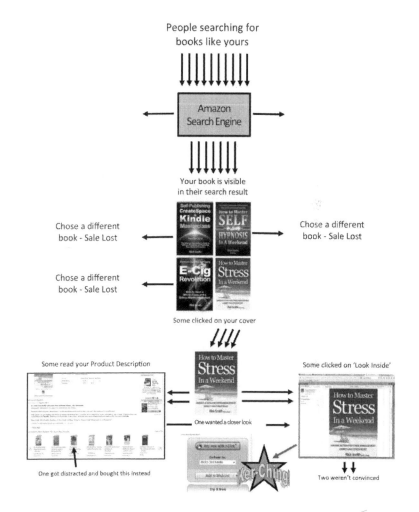

People searching for books like yours

Amazon Search Engine

Your book is visible in their search result

Chose a different book - Sale Lost

Chose a different book - Sale Lost

Chose a different book - Sale Lost

Some clicked on your cover

Some read your Product Description

Some clicked on 'Look Inside'

One wanted a closer look

One got distracted and bought this instead

Two weren't convinced

If you've come across Sales Funnels in the past, you'll understand that there are lots of customers flooding onto the Amazon site all the time, and those that are searching for books like yours have to make lightning fast decisions, mainly based on first-impressions and gut-instinct, to sort the few books they have time to investigate from the twenty or more that are on their screen. If they're looking for expert advice, you need to look like an expert, and a shabby cover won't capture anyone's attention.

As you can clearly see from the Sales Funnel diagram, your Cover is front-and-center in three out of five decision-to-buy *elimination tests*. A great cover can dramatically increase those click-through rates and propel more buyers over the finishing line.

Color

In the previous example, we highlighted the role of color in drawing attention to your cover. In *stress,* which bridges both *health* and *self-help* categories, soothing blue and green covers are very popular. So you have a choice; you either follow the crowd on palette, or you go for pure visual impact. There's nothing intrinsically wrong with this cover strategy, but you have just seen a good example of getting it wrong.

I recommend a free web service called **colorlovers.com.** Most people aren't trained or capable of selecting a color palette based on one or two basic shades. Designers know how to do this, but if you want to be able to choose four or five color options to use on your book cover, try it. Colorlovers works particularly well if you're using a photograph as the basis for your cover. You can select the dominant color, or a highlight you want to accentuate, and color lover will build you a palette of matched colors, which will work. You can then use these for font and type effects, color bands, or any other element of your cover design, without concern about whether you're causing a clash.

There's more advice and information about choosing color palettes and type effects in the next section.

How to Approach Cover Design

Here's a great video that shows how the professionals work on covers at the big publishing houses. I recommend you make time to watch it, because it will show you the main considerations that the big Publishers use to make their books catch the eye.

http://www.youtube.com/watch?v=l2Z86L25v3o

For you, there are several ways to approach Cover Design:

Amazon Cover Creator Resources

Both KDP and Createspace have online Cover Creator wizards that you can use free when you're publishing a book. The advantage of these is that they're correctly sized, and all you have to do is choose a style, insert your text, and maybe exchange the image for one you have on your computer or you bought online from Shutterstock or Fotolia, and you can have a professional looking cover, up and running in a few minutes.

The minor downside is that thousands of other people have used variants of the same design for their covers too. Given that there are over 14 million titles on Amazon, it's unlikely that one of these books will randomly show up anywhere near yours, and possibly not even in the same category, but it could happen. However, for free it's probably a risk worth taking if you're short of time, skills, or money.

But, to be honest, they're not very exciting.

Fiverr.com **www.fiverr.com**

If you haven't already come across Fiverr.com, it's a website where thousands of craftsmen and women, from graphic designers to animators to voice over artists, offer their basic service for $5.00. This may sound ridiculously cheap, but the salary for a designer in India, where there are plenty of very skilled creative freelancers, is less than one tenth of that for someone in the US or Western Europe, so that's the equivalent of $50 an hour, which is about the time they will spend on your job.

The good ones turn out great work and they're really quick, because they have to do a lot of jobs to earn a living. However, if you can manage some of the wacky communications issues, and give good clear briefs to your freelancer, you'll usually get a decent product. I especially like Fiverr.com when I want some really quick Photoshopping done; stuff that would take me an hour or two to figure out. I have one re-toucher who turns a simple job around in ten minutes, which is better than you'd get from your company's internal art department!

There are lots of artists offering book-cover design on Fiverr.com. You could try a few, or alternately you could ask on a couple of Facebook Groups for recommendations, so that you can see real live versions of your potential freelancer's work. As always, it's important to send a tight brief. Make sure your text is unambiguous and accurate, because a designer won't correct your spelling errors. They'll just make your mistakes look nice on the page!

When you brief your designer, it's a good idea to send four or five cover shots, clipped from Amazon, of book covers that you want to take style cues from. You can tell your designer you like a particular color palette, even an image, and of course the layout. A smart designer will do you two or three quick treatments and if you choose one, then it's a good idea to buy another five bucks of their time, which ensures they finish your choice properly and you get an even better job. By using this low-cost system, you can even audition several designers on the same project and you'll have ten or twelve covers to choose from.

Elance and ODesk

Next up are the big freelance sites, Elance.com and ODesk.com. On these sites, once you register as a client (which is free) and fill in your payment information so that all the agreed transactions are automated, you can post a brief for anything you want. If you load the search keyword 'book cover designer' or 'Kindle cover designer' you will get plenty of responses. In your brief, apart from a description of your book, including the genre, you should request thumbnail samples of their work. Some of them may have websites you can look at, so ask for links.

Shortlist the ones you like, perhaps three, and offer them a 'pitch fee', which is a little freelance contract so you can sample their ideas. Typically a good contractor will want between $5 and $12 an hour, so my recommendation is that you offer them two-hour fee to produce three ideas in rough. Tell them it's a contest between three designers. This time you may spend around $50 to get back nine ideas from which to choose.

Some people like to put out their shortlist covers on Facebook and hold a beauty contest. I've seen a lot of these posts and they rarely seem to form any consensus; people are all over the place.

If you don't trust your own judgment, put your favorite three covers on your smartphone, and show them to a few people who (you know) like to read the genre of book you're writing. Just drop it into the conversation when you've had a few drinks to loosen up, and you can expect to get a lot more information about peoples' real likes and dislikes in a real bar than you will in a Facebook comment bar.

When you choose the one you like, award a new contract to the winner to produce your cover. You should order a Kindle version, a Createspace version for your paperback, and a 3D version for you to use on things like Facebook posts. You should specifically ask for the following files as the final delivery:

- Kindle cover in the native design format (whichever graphics program the designer used)
- Kindle cover as a high-quality JPG file.
- Createspace Cover in the native design format.
- Createspace Cover as a flattened PDF
- 3D Cover as a PNG file, so you can paste it into promotional material.

These will cover all your bases. You should state in the conditions of your freelance offer that copyright of all materials will be yours once you pay for the job. You need the files because if you decide to make changes in the future, you don't necessarily want to be locked into one designer. You should always keep consistency between your Kindle Cover and your Createspace cover, if you are publishing in paperback. If you update one, make sure you update the other. Search likes consistency.

How much should you offer?

My view on this is that you must balance what the job is *really worth to you* against the quality and attention you want your freelancer to give it. These guys thrive on repeat business, so they'll always try to do the best job they can, but of course the more time you give them, the better the result you'll get back.

My own strategy is to offer them four or maybe five hours work, depending on the complexity of the job. I have heard of people that scalp their freelancers by paying for two hours, but I'd rather have someone who takes care of my work because I'm slightly over-compensating them, than that they rush it because I'm screwing them. People tell me that I'm contributing to wage inflation in the emerging markets. You know what, I don't care.

Even if the price doubled every three years, it would still be a while before it became uneconomic, and why shouldn't people who contribute to the success of your business be rewarded for their contribution, as you work with them? The extra twenty bucks is nothing to you, given what you're getting for your money. But to a young college student in Ukraine or India it could buy the textbook he needs for his next exams. Treat your freelancers well, and they'll do a better job.

By the way, if you're nervous about running freelancers, don't be. The ODesk and Elance dashboards are very well laid out and really simple to use. Communication with your freelancer is via e-mail, which is all run through the dashboard, so there's no direct contact between you. Your freelancer will file progress reports online if needed, and you can pay for the job either all at the end, or in stages. If you set up the payment stages at the beginning, the dashboard takes care of making the payments on time and charges your account. There is a full range of support services, including complaints procedures.

Crowdsourcing

This is the most exciting option, but also potentially the most expensive. One of the best examples is at 99designs.com, who have handled over 100,000 graphic design projects this way.

Basically, you brief your cover project online, again giving a description of the genre, and maybe the Product Description you're going to use on your Amazon Sales Page, to tell them what the book is about. Your brief then goes out to a fixed number of designers, depending on the package you choose. The cheapest option is £199 and gets you around thirty designers working on your project. You can pay extra for more designers, but frankly you're already going to get 30 almost-finished covers back, and you're bound to like at least one of them. If you can write a brief, it's up to you how much guidance you inject. My recommendation is to take a chance, and let them have the whole idea on their own.

Just a note: you may find that you have to pay your chosen designer extra to produce both your Kindle and your Createspace covers.

Specialist Online Designer

There are many freelance designers on the web who ply their trade based mainly on recommendation. Tracking down a good one is a matter of posting out on your Facebook Author Groups and asking your friends and other members. Everyone's getting their covers done somewhere, so you'll get lots of response from a busy group. Most posters will put a link in their post so you'll quickly be able to see the quality of the recommended designer's work portfolio.

Unlike Crowdsourcing, you'll have to stay in touch with the process, because you'll probably be seeing and selecting from rough ideas along the way. Expect to pay $75-$250.

Dedicated Graphic Designer

If you're writing for vanity, or if you have a good graphic designer in the family, this is the ultimate luxury. A cover that's custom designed for you, by someone who gets directly involved at your idea stage. Face to face. You get a broad communications channel to convey your hopes and dreams for your book, and to enthuse the designer in the process.

Good designers work fast, so a book cover won't take them long in front of the screen. But the time they spend talking to you and showing you ideas, and waiting for your approvals, all has to be paid for. So it's not unusual to run into four figures for a design job, if you aren't sure what you want right from the start. For a working author trying to build a business from nothing, a dedicated designer is a luxury you can store away for later, when you're on the New York Times Bestseller List.

Do It Yourself

If you have any flair for art or graphics, then you should relish the opportunity to try designing your own covers. Apart from your writing, it might be another aspect of your creativity, which you can begin to develop. The software available in the market today is terrific, and not expensive. Adobe Photoshop Elements or Microsoft Publisher are both great tools for cover design and cost less than $150, which, for something you will use time after time to save a lot of money, is good value.

Both these have free equivalents. The nearest equivalent to Photoshop is Gimp. If you download it, make sure you get a reputable download site and you have your antivirus scanning on, because these free programs are notorious for adding malware to your computer.

On the Mac, Pages, which you may well be using as your writing software, is also a very capable publishing program and you can build book covers in a similar way to MS Publisher.

If you have a basic grasp of the software, but you're lacking ideas, just browse the Amazon bookstore until you find a few covers you like. It would be wrong to copy someone else's work, both morally and legally, but you can choose color palettes, see different ways of achieving impact with type, and get a great feel for what displays well on the page. Take those cues and experiment for yourself.

Another great place to look for ideas is on iTunes or Netflix. Film posters are really powerful marketing weapons, but these days, because of the user interface on TV streaming and download services, they have to do a similar job as book covers on Amazon; they have to jump off your screen even when they're very small. So, design has evolved to make these posters work the same way.

If you're not too computer-savvy, or even if you are, set up a folder to store your favorite images in, and clip them from your screen ('save image as') so you have a *light box* of ideas of things you like, each time you're trying to come up with a new cover concept.

Microsoft Publisher: The Professional Design Tool that Beginners Love

My personal choice for a design tool is Microsoft Publisher. I make no apology for expressing a preference here, and I would recommend Publisher for anyone who is serious about doing their own covers but doesn't have much graphics experience, even none at all. I find Photoshop too expensive, heavy and complex. Photoshop Elements isn't simple as a design tool because it's mainly aimed at the digital photo market.

Publisher is very quick to learn if you've used other Microsoft programs, particularly Word and PowerPoint.

Click here to get the extended version of this Stunning Covers Section, which gives step-by step instructions, with screen-shots, on designing covers with Microsoft Publisher: **http://tiny.cc/gxsknx**

The link is repeated at the end of the book.

Chapter Three Summary

- Your Cover has a massive impact on getting your initial visitor to investigate and buy your book.
- Covers should be sympathetic to the landscape of the genre, but distinguish themselves using slick design and fast-scan readability.
- Titles must be easily readable in thumbnail view.
- Don't unnecessarily shock your readers (unless you're publishing vampire books).
- Use a proper color palette.
- Use fiverr.com to get lots of good ideas, for cheap.
- Use freelancers to get a higher-quality job, if your book justifies the investment.
- Have a go, and see how you get on. You might surprise yourself!

Chapter 4 - Product Description

Your *Product Description* is yours to control. A great one will resonate with the casual browser, and give them a reason to look further into your package. A bad one will turn them straight off and they'll go somewhere else, and probably buy a different book.

If this is your first try at publishing on Amazon, you'll be prompted to enter your Product Description as a part of the information you enter about your book on the first page of the *Add New Title* dashboard.

The objective is to write a compelling passage which appeals to someone looking for a book in your niche, then display it in a way which looks professional, and in keeping with the person's expectations of the quality of your book. If it looks good and it reads well, it will push more clicks to your *Look Inside* section. The more people you push this way, the more sales you'll make.

Your Product Description is also an excellent opportunity to place long-tail (less common and less competitive) keyword phrases where the Amazon Search Engine can find them.

Think Like Your Customer

To understand the importance your Product Description (sometimes referred to as *Blurb*) you need think like your potential customer. If they're reading your Product Description, it means they've done their initial search and chosen your book, based on its title and cover, and clicked through take a closer look.

This is gold dust for an Amazon author. Once a potential buyer gets to your Sales Page, they have probably made a decision to *buy* a book, and yours is a serious contender for their hard earned cash. Now your job is to convert them and make them hit the *"Buy Now With One Click"* button, so the deal is sealed.

So long as your Reviews are in decent shape, your Book Description carries enormous weight. For fiction and non-fiction writers alike, it is the most important and best opportunity you have to sell your book's content and messages, so you must pay close attention to it.

Check Your Competitors

Before you set about writing your Product Description, it's always a good idea to take a look at your competitors, and see how they've handled it. When you look at other Sales Pages, you'll notice two distinctly different types of layout for the Book Description.

Advanced Formatting

Some Product Descriptions will contain advanced formatting, such as orange colored headers, italics, bullet-lists and bold type. If done properly, these formatting additions can be very appealing, and will help boost your conversion rate, because readers naturally associate such sophistication with big publishers, which adds untold credibility. Text formatting can also be used to draw the eye to important statements in your Product Description.

The bad news is that the only way to achieve this kind of formatting is to insert HTML code inside the text when you're managing your book's information during the upload or revision process. I said at the beginning of this book that you wouldn't need HTML in order to publish great books on Amazon, however if you want to format your Book Description in this way, it's unavoidable. The good news is that there are plenty of people who can do this for you at very low cost, for example on fiverr.com. Alternately you can do it yourself if you're careful, even if you have no HTML knowledge at all. In October 2013, Amazon made some changes to the HTML tags they will support, so if you get it done externally, you should ensure that your contractor is up with the latest play. The full list of Amazon-supported HTML tags is available here:

https://kdp.amazon.com/help?topicId=A1JPU WCSD6F59O

The best news is that there is a fantastic software tool called *Better Book Tools* (**www.betterbooktools.com**), which costs $47 for the complete suite. This program converts your Product Description text into Amazon-approved HTML without you needing any HTML knowledge whatsoever. The software also includes some excellent supplementary tools for keyword search and comparison, but for the

HTML conversion alone I recommend you check it out. I am not affiliated to this company.

Alternately, get it done on fiverr.com. Just bear in mind that if you start publishing more books you'll be changing your Product Description all the time, as you run promotions and update information, so those five buck gigs will soon start adding up and you'll want to be able to do it yourself.

However, not all the big books use this rich text method, as you'll see if you take a look at J K Rowling's *The Casual Vacancy*, which has a Book Description which is done exactly as you will do yours if you just type (or preferably prepare offline then copy/paste) into the Kindle upload screen.

How Long Should Your Description Be?

Your Book Description can be up to 4000 characters. Some gurus advise you to use it all, and some say keep it short, especially for fiction writers.

Realistically, you need to use just as much as is necessary to close the sale. If your Kindle price is low (say 99c - $2.99), the potential customer is in an *impulse purchase* frame of mind, and will click through to buy your book once they've crossed the threshold of being convinced that it's worth the tiny financial risk. Conversely, if your price is high (say $4.99 and upwards), they may take more convincing, so the longer you can keep your potential reader engaged, the deeper you will immerse them in your book's 'culture' and the more likely they will buy it.

The exception is if you manage to turn them off with ridiculous claims or bad grammar, which is a cardinal sin in your Book Description. If you have any suspicions about your own competence, you should ask for help and get someone you trust to check your Product Description before you upload it. Bad blurb will send your buyers scurrying away, and there are lots of temptations scattered around your Sales Page for them to click through to something else.

What to Write

Here are some general points you should employ for both Fiction and Non-Fiction Book Descriptions.

Think Like a Publisher

Write your book description as if you're a copywriter who's been hired to do the job. You've read the book (goodness knows you've certainly done that) so you should understand everything about it, but you also need to step outside the process for a moment and describe the book as if you're trying to sell it to somebody. It's all too easy to be so immersed in your own work that you lose your objectivity. You must write your Product Description in the third person (unless you're already well-known in your field), and you must tell the reader only what they need to know in order to convert the sale.

Stay Away From Detail

Your job is to intrigue and entice the reader, not to give them a short-course in what you've written. It's invaluable to see what your competitors are doing. As a short cut, there's nothing wrong with copy/pasting the Product Description from a book you admire into your Word Processor, and then changing each sentence one at a time so that the underlying structure and flow are maintained, but the plot, content and characters are yours. Model success, always.

Grab Your Buyer

Grab your buyer at the start and always leave them wanting more. The first and last lines of your Product Description are the most valuable, and you should spend the most time on these. I'm sure, especially if you've written a thriller, you've been through this process for the first sentence of your book, so get into that mindset again and write a devastating opening line.

Close the Deal

Always end your Product Description with a *call to action*. In every kind of selling situation, potential buyers need to be told to *do something* or they'll often carry on browsing somewhere else. This is called *decision support* and you shouldn't omit it. There's more about this at the end of this section.

Fiction Descriptions 101

I'm not much of a fiction writer (well not yet anyway, I have to pay the bills first) so I've gone out to the wider world to see what the experts advise is the best way to approach fiction blurb. Here's my interpretation of what I learned;

Set the Scene Powerfully: *"When Rick Smith sat down to write once more on that fateful Monday Morning, little did he know the maelstrom of chaos that was about to unfold in the days ahead..."*

Briefly Introduce your Key Antagonists, Scale, and Environment: *"Ten thousand miles away in the Australian Outback, evil forces were preparing to unleash events of catastrophic dimensions that would change Smith's world forever..."*

Link It All Together: *"Unwittingly catapulted onto an explosive trajectory that would see his very soul pulled apart, as he struggled to contain a terrifying sequence of events that threatened to destroy not only him, but the entire New Malden Book Club..."*

And Summarize: *"How would it all end, or could it really end at all?"*

Did you see what I did there? OK, that might not be the best fiction blurb ever written, but I'm sure you get the drift, and if you look at a few more Book Descriptions in your specific genre, you should find it much easier to come up with a good one of your own!

Non-Fiction Descriptions 101

Writing a non-fiction Product Description is completely different. Here you're trying to convince your reader that they'll be making the best possible decision by buying your book, in order to answer the question or solve the problem that brought them to Amazon in the first place. You need to get inside the mind of your customer, and ask yourself the same questions.

Here's a break-down of the Product Description structure I've used for my book *"Master Self-Hypnosis in a Weekend"* which is in a highly competitive sector and is sitting high up on the first page in Amazon:

Why My Book Is Better Than the Others (the Passive/Aggressive Approach):

"Hundreds of books have been published about Self-Hypnosis, so what makes this one special? Well, maybe you're trying Self-Hypnosis for the first time, or maybe you've tried before and failed. Whatever the case, you're looking for results, otherwise you'll probably waste a lot of time, and come away disappointed and disillusioned. You need a System."

Clarity of Explanation and Implied Guarantee of Results:

"In 'How to Master Self-Hypnosis in a Weekend' professional hypnotist Rick Smith demonstrates a step-by-step system which anyone can use to succeed."

—

What's In the Package?:

"Everything you need, included freely downloadable script recordings, is provided. Using this book, you will quickly master the key Self-Hypnosis techniques that enable you to drop easily and quickly into a comfortable trance anywhere, anytime."

How You Will Benefit:

"You'll also learn how to use your new Self-Hypnosis skills for relaxation and recreation, how to use Self-Hypnosis to control stress and to center yourself professionally, how to attack bad habits, such as smoking, drinking, over-eating, in fact anything that you feel the need to change, and how to empower yourself for motivation, focus and commitment."

The Short-Cuts That Will Save You Time/Money/Frustration:

"You'll also discover how to avoid the common mistakes that other people make:

- *they don't practice often enough, so they fail to master the key techniques;*
- *they don't get the 'set-up' right, so they become distracted; they cling on to their inhibitions, so they never release their restrictive self-control;*
- *and they try to analyze too much, rather than allowing nature do its best work."*

How It Will Be For You Once You Have Read It:

"If you follow these step-by-step instructions you will quickly learn everything you need to know in order to master the simple skills of Self-Hypnosis. With regular use, you will acquire a powerful secret weapon that will serve you in almost any aspect of your life. And the more you do it, the better you will become."

Sign Off:

"It's easy, it's quick, and it's really fun to do! "

You can use bullet-point or numbered lists for some of your factual statements, but you'll need to use the simple HTML tricks to get them to display well. You should also add a Call to Action such as *"Buy it Now"*, or *"Click on 'Look Inside' to Find Out More"*

You'll also notice a liberal sprinkling of Keywords throughout this Product Description. On no account be tempted to write a long list of keywords and put it at the bottom. This is such an obvious attempt to game the system that I am convinced the Amazon 'crawler' that indexes your book will largely ignore it

If you are inexperienced as a writer or communicator, it's a great idea to give it to someone else to read. The simple questions you're asking are: *"Do You Get It?"* and *"Would You Buy It?"* Make them read it in front of you, and only once or twice, because that's the way that your potential customers will read it, and they won't dig in to discover deep meanings. You only get one shot with an Amazon customer, so you'd better make it count.

Although it sounds obvious, just run it through your spelling and grammar checker before you post it on the site. You won't be the first person who unwittingly published an accidental howler, and it will definitely be spotted by someone.

Chapter Four Summary

- Your Product Description enables potential buyers to make their decision to *Buy* or *Look Inside.*
- A shabby Product Description will send buyers elsewhere.
- Always write your Product Description in the third person. It is not your autobiography.
- Emulate Product Descriptions from books you admire. Use their layout and flow, and your own details, characters, or key points.
- Use HTML formatted Product Descriptions for a more professional look.
- Write only as much as you need to get your reader's commitment.
- Make sure your grammar and spelling are flawless.

Chapter 5 – Reviews

Reviews perform a number of key functions, all of which add up to extra 'points' for your book in the Search Results. Our two different kinds of optimization, the effect in the Search Engine, and the effect on the audience's buying decision, are covered by the various aspects of Amazon's Reviews. So why are Reviews so important?

If you owned an Internet sales business (maybe you do) you would probably pay close attention to the quality of the products you sell, because that would be an important factor in your success or failure. However, because Amazon has thrown open its sales platform to anyone who has something to sell, it's impossible for them to quality control all the products passing through their ecosystem, especially when it comes to books. Frankly, there's some utter dross on the Kindle Bookstore, and occasionally you may get suckered into buying and downloading a real turkey.

So Amazon's way of dealing with the quality control aspects for Kindle (and physical) books, is to let the market self-regulate, and that happens through the Review System. If you know all about the Review format, you might skip ahead, but if you've never encountered it before, here's how it works and how important it is to respect it when it comes to your book(s).

Anyone can review any product on Amazon, and the *moderation filters*, that is to say the rules for allowing or blocking a review, are quite loose. Just like the Sales Ranking system, there's a ranking algorithm built into the Review system, which is much more sophisticated than it appears. Each review earns between one and five stars, and after a few reviews have been acquired, the average review is shown up-top next to the Book Title so that people can instantly scan to see the apparent quality of the book. Opinion is divided about the relevance of Reviews on your Sales Ranking. But what's for sure is that having no reviews at all will ensure you're book languishes precisely nowhere in any kind of ranking at all.

The Amazon review system is smart enough to pick up on some popular scams, such as the same people constantly giving five star reviews to the same authors, and even (anecdotally) a pass/fail check on reviews which come from Amazon account holders whose physical address is the same as the author (such as a wife reviewing her husband's book, even if she legitimately bought and read it). Nevertheless, there are gaps in the system, and if you search around to find the highest ranked Reviewers, some of them don't even post real language in their reviews, just character groups or gibberish. I cannot adequately express how angry I get when I see this kind of thing!

There's an alternative world of Top-Reviewers on Amazon, driven by the sheer number of reviews they've posted, and the number of helpful votes their reviews attract. It's highly competitive, and if can get your book reviewed by a really high-ranking Amazon reviewer, it will be beneficial for your book's performance. If you are promoting a novel, I'm told that chasing these reviews can really work well.

For most niche non-fiction, it's unlikely to be a successful strategy.

Amazon Verified Purchase

Any review you acquire is valid, but the most valuable are *Amazon Verified Purchase* reviews, which are posted by people who actually bought the product. Reviews are very important, both *artistically*, to persuade browsers that your book is worthy of their money, and *technically*, for raising you up the Rankings ladder, so it is to be respected and handled with care.

If you write a good book, and people like it, you will get good reviews and these will help you on many levels to become more successful. If you write a bad book, especially if it's perceived as poor value, the Reviewers will hammer you, and you'll be out of business. If you meet some peoples' expectations but not others, you may get a few poor reviews, but this is part of being in the creative business, so suck it up and move on. Whatever you do, never try to engage directly with a Reviewer, even if they cane you. If a Review is grossly unfair or seriously offensive, you can ask Amazon Customer Services to investigate and take it down, in

—

75

which case the Reviewer may have their account blocked, so flame wars rarely happen on Amazon Reviews.

Why Reviews Are Important To You

Reviews lend credibility, and *social proof* to your book, and tell prospective purchasers what other people thought about it. Remember the *Wisdom of Crowds* mantra that crops up time and time again? Once they are in their chosen search category, people will rely on others' experiences to tell them if your book is worthwhile. Once they're reading your reviews, most of them have made a purchasing commitment to buy a book on the subject, and the quality of your reviews will exert serious influence towards whether they buy yours. Review *quality* is up there with the quality of your Product Description as a key decision factor for your customers, so you need to focus on getting some good ones.

Another reason why Reviews are critical is because they're an important component of your search visibility. The balance between quality and quantity of reviews is unclear, but you can be sure that your average star rating is pretty important. There are other factors, like whether many people have clicked on the '*I found this review useful*' button, which also has the effect of raising popular reviews up the list and dropping unpopular ones down until they may eventually disappear completely.

—

In the medium-sized niches that most non-fiction authors write for, just six or seven decent reviews will be enough to populate your Sales Page. Reviews are equally as important for Fiction as Non-Fiction, except that a moneymaking fiction title may need upwards of fifty or sixty reviews before it's making the royalties commensurate with the effort expended. Fiction genres are generally much more competitive than non-fiction, and the commitment to read and review a fiction book might run into days, rather than hours for non-fiction.

Based on my own experiences, around fifty good (five and four-star) reviews will provide tremendous support for your book in Search, and ensure it stays in the top few rows, even if sales fluctuate. For this reason alone, it's well worth the effort of hustling for as many reviews as you can get, from wherever you can legitimately obtain them. Ten in the first month, and fifty in the first year, are good targets to aim for.

Getting Your First Reviews

The blogosphere is full of debate about what is considered ethical or unethical about getting reviews for a newly launched book. I deliberately stay out of the debate because I believe that quality will ultimately shine through. As Barack Obama famously said, *"You can put lipstick on a pig, (but) it's still a pig"*.

If your book is good, and you get a little help to bring it to the attention of an appreciative public, you may simply be leveling the field against the marketing muscle of the big publishers, as long as no laws are broken and the spirit of fair play isn't violated. Some say that asking friends to buy your book and review it is a perfectly reasonable tactic, as long as you don't influence or coerce them into stating anything in the review that is knowingly false or misleading. You should not write reviews for your own book, of course.

Stick to the Rules

Amazon has rules (the Terms of Service, or TOS), and these are constantly changing so you should familiarize yourself with the latest version through the Kindle or Createspace websites.

Good and Bad Practice

Whatever you do, don't buy reviews online, from places like fiverr.com (although there are other excellent author services available there). You'll almost certainly be voiding Amazons rules, and if they get a sniff of something untoward, you could find all your reviews deleted and even your book suspended from sale.

You should most definitely be asking your readers to review your book by placing requests in the front and back matter of your manuscript, on your website or blog (if you have one) and anywhere else that's appropriate.

Once you gain some momentum, and your book starts to sell under its own steam, you will pick up natural reviews, and the better and more life-changing your book, the more people will be inspired to review you. If you should be fortunate enough to get *professional* reviews, based on books you send out to magazines or media outlets, make sure you get the reviewer to post on Amazon, or get their permission to place the review in your Product Description.

In general, you can never have too many reviews (as long as they are good ones) so make a structured plan as soon as you're ready to launch your book, and don't stop promoting and pushing until you've got your five to seven reviews on each major Amazon Sales Page.

Chapter Five Summary

- Reviews count towards your book's overall visibility in Search. More reviews are better than less.
- Your average Review score is a factor in how you book ranks for position in each search. All things being equal, the book with the higher average score will do better.
- *Amazon Verified Reviews* are the most valuable.
- Hustle and nag people to review your book quickly: you need six or seven early reviews to populate your Sales page.
- Don't break Amazon's rules; you may find reviews deleted and even have your books banned.
- Target ten reviews in your book's first month, and fifty in the first year.

Your Checklist

So, there we are. You now understand the importance of Optimization and the benefits of paying attention to it before you put your book up for sale on Amazon. Here's a reminder, in the form of a checklist you should use for every book;

Keywords

Use the Amazon website and any other tools you have to develop a short-list of ten solid keywords which will attract search traffic to your book. Decide which ones are going in your title, and reserve seven for your metadata.

Titles and Subtitles

Develop strong, keyword-rich Titles and Subtitles. Try to use your strongest keyword early in your main title, and weave keywords and phrases into your subtitle.

Stunning Covers

Invest time and effort into a great cover. Make sure it works properly in thumbnail view. It should both blend in and stand out on the Search Results screen. You have only a fleeting moment to grab your potential buyer visually.

Product Description

Take your time, and make it good. Follow the pattern of successful books in your genre, and use HTML formatting to make your Product Description look professional. Ruthlessly edit; you must capture your readers' attention quickly. Strategically scatter your keywords and long tail phrases in your Product Description.

Reviews

Use all legitimate means to acquire reviews as fast as possible. Target ten in the first month, fifty in the first year. Be proactive and persistent. Include *keyword-buy* instructions when you are communicating with reviewers online.

In Summary

If you pay attention to each of these five key optimization elements, your book will outperform most other books in it's category, simply because many self-publishers don't bother.

It's a tiny effort in comparison to actually writing your book, and it shouldn't take you more than a day to set everything up. Apart from seeking reviews, everything else simply requires monitoring and tweaking as you begin to understand how your book is working in the market, and you start to get some feedback from the reviews themselves.

—

It's a good idea to take a look at your metadata keywords from time to time, because some may simply not work (maybe there's too much competition) and you can try new ones any time you like.

Never be afraid to redesign your cover, either. Keep a close eye on new books appearing in your search results, and see what the successful ones are doing that's giving them visibility.

Remember the objective of optimization: to make your book easy to find so that it naturally shows up in as many places as possible.

More eyeballs = more clicks = more sales = more royalties.

Additional Resources

Books You Should Read

There are literally thousands of Self-Publishing guides in the market. Pretty much every self-published author writes one at some stage, and many of them are decidedly average, or at the very least repetitive. I should know; I've read them all.

This list is by no means exhaustive as far as the good ones go, but if you only read these books, you would have covered around 99% of the information that's out there.

Platform by Michael Hyatt

Hyatt is a massively successful Social Media Strategy blogger with a huge following. This seminal book lays out strategies to build a far-reaching platform, which can be harnessed to deliver a willing audience for anything you write. There are some grand concepts in here, and not all of it is useful, however a new Author will find some great observations on human nature in general and consumer behavior in particular.

Make Your Book Work Harder by Nancy Hendrickson & Michelle Campbell-Scott

I keep Nancy and Michelle's fantastic book permanently in the top row of my Kindle Library on my iPad,

---

because there's barely a week goes by that I don't feel the need to consult it. This book is packed full of great advice for Indie Authors, such as how to get on to other e-book platforms, how to do an audiobook with ACX, and some really cool stuff abut Social Media campaigns and Book Promotion opportunities.

Make a Killing on Kindle
by Michael Alvear

For me, this is one of the best books currently in print about Book Marketing for independent authors. Michael Alvear is a successful Amazon author in his own right, and this book will give you many great tactics to drive your sales, with not much effort and zero cost. A must-read.

Createspace and Kindle Self-Publishing Matrix by Chris Naish

If you really want to drill down into keyword strategies, this book is the blueprint. I must admit a bias here, because Chris Naish used my book as the central case study when he was formulating his Matrix (he calls me Agent Smith). If you like the analytical approach to marketing, this is the book for you. If you get keywords right, your book will do things you never expected.

The Kindle Publishing Bible by Tom Corson-Knowles

Corson-Knowles is one of the new gurus of the self-publishing business, and all his books are worthy of your attention. This one leads with some great advice on titles and keywords, and lots of solid Marketing advice for newcomers.

Pictures on Kindle by Aaron Shepard

Aaron is undoubtedly my favorite Author Geek, and all his technical books are worth their weight in gold when you're learning your way around Kindle publishing. This one is particularly noteworthy because it completely demystifies the process of getting pictures and graphics to display well on all Kindle devices, which is far from simple. He also has two others I would recommend: *From Word to Kindle,* and *HTML Fixes for Kindle.* Pure gold.

Is 99c the New Free? by Steve Scott

Scott is another of the well-known gurus in this market, and this book, a relatively recent publication, gives a great explanation of why 99c pricing is better for your business than free promotion, and how to use it effectively.

Facebook Groups

There are lots of Authors and Self-Publishers' Facebook Groups which you can choose from. Some of the better ones are real thriving communities for independents like you, and there you can learn advanced techniques very quickly, ask questions, and generally interact with experienced authors who are usually only too happy to pass on what they know. Try to avoid Groups that only seem to have pages of self-promotion, particularly for free books, because these will clog up your Newsfeed with useless stuff.

Two that I recommend are as follows:

The Fab Friday 99 Cents Promotion Group for Authors **https://www.facebook.com/groups/200905610 068048/**
and

Kindle Publishing Bible --
https://www.facebook.com/groups/KindlePubli shers/

These are closed groups, and you will need to apply to join. However, they contain quality people and the moderators ensure that junk promotional material never makes it to the main feed.

And here is a more complete list:

Pat's First Kindle Book --
https://www.facebook.com/groups/3571123310 27292/

---

99 cent Kindle Deals --
https://www.facebook.com/groups/2156813985 01172/
99¢ Kindle Book Promotion --
https://www.facebook.com/groups/198597020 319359/
Page One Profits Kindle Group --
https://www.facebook.com/groups/pageonepro fits/
Author's Forum --
https://www.facebook.com/groups/AuthorsFor um01/
Self Publish Bootcamp --
https://www.facebook.com/groups/selfpublish bootcamp/
Wicked Simple K --
https://www.facebook.com/groups/387202538 033195/
Author Meeting Place --
https://www.facebook.com/groups/authormeet ingplace/
Authors, Agents, and Aspiring Writers --
https://www.facebook.com/groups/204725947 524/
Author Exchange --
https://www.facebook.com/groups/200396383 343774/
Writers' Group --
https://www.facebook.com/groups/membersw ritersgroup/

The Literary Lounge --
https://www.facebook.com/groups/1354861331
30440/
Literary Discussion Group – We promote ourselves --
https://www.facebook.com/groups/AuthorsAn
dReviews/
Books, Books, and more Books!!! --
https://www.facebook.com/groups/320356974
732142/
Kindle Publishers --
https://www.facebook.com/groups/512098985
483106/
Ebook Review Club --
https://www.facebook.com/groups/1230947811
81179/
Kindle Marketing Revelations Insiders --
https://www.facebook.com/groups/kindlemark
etingrevelations/
Authors Promoting Authors --
https://www.facebook.com/groups/apablog/
Book Promotion --
https://www.facebook.com/groups/BookPromo
tion/
Next Top Author --
https://www.facebook.com/groups/nexttopaut
hor/
Kindle Publishing Bible --
https://www.facebook.com/groups/KindlePubli
shers/
Marketing for Authors --

https://www.facebook.com/groups/1468136121 65228/

The Fab Friday 99 Cents Promotion Group for Authors
https://www.facebook.com/groups/200905610 068048/

Subscribe to my Self-Publishing Masterclass Newsletter and Download "Stunning Covers" for Free

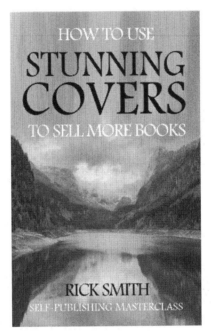

Just use this the Link: **http://tiny.cc/gxsknx**

Please feel free to e-mail me with any suggestions or criticisms, to **mailto:rick@spmasterclass.com**

Read on to find out about more Self Publishing Masterclass books by Rick Smith

CreateSpace
&
Kindle
Self-Publishing
Masterclass

Second Edition
New for 2015

**The Step-by-Step Author's Guide to
Writing, Publishing and Marketing
Your Books on Amazon**

Rick Smith

More than 5000 Copies Sold – Now in its Second Edition for 2015 and Beyond.

"Probably the Most Complete New Author Guide on the Market Today"

Hundreds of books have been written about Self-Publishing, so what makes this one special? Well, maybe you're Writing and Publishing for the first time, or maybe you've done the hard part and you need to know how to get your Masterpiece out there and into the hands of a real audience? Whatever the case, you're looking for *results* otherwise you'll probably waste a lot of time, and come away disappointed and disillusioned. **You need a System.**

Step-By-Step - Amazon's Paperback and E-Book Publishing Systems Explained

In *CreateSpace and Kindle Self-Publishing Masterclass,* top-selling independent author Rick Smith demonstrates a logical, step-by-step system which new Authors can use to succeed. This book will fast-track you through the Jungle!

Writing, Publishing, and Marketing Your Books

Here you'll find the truth about what to write and how to get it finished. You'll learn the **16 Golden Rules for Successful Amazon Authors.** You'll be shown the important things that must be done correctly, and the other stuff which just slows you down.

- Why you should publish both Paperback and Kindle formats
- Why you should always do Createspace first
- What are the best software tools for organization, creativity, and productivity?
- How to create or source amazing low-cost covers that drive your sales
- How to build world-class Sales Pages on Amazon's storefront, with no technical skills required   In fact, everything you'll need to take your book to market.

Marketing 101 for New Independent Authors

You'll also discover the right moves to achieve commercial success for your book;

- Where to find your first willing customers who'll kick-off your sales
- The importance of Reviews and how to get genuine customers to write them
- Using the right Keyword tactics to get your book onto Page 1 in Amazon's Category Search
- How to price, track, and promote your book, and when to write the next one

As you follow these step-by-step instructions you'll quickly learn **everything you need to know** in order to start a new career as an Independent Self-Published Author. Along the way, you'll acquire a few Secret Weapons that could propel your book to it's Category's

Top-Row, where every author wants to be and every potential buyer can see you. *Publishing your first book is the ride of your life; get it right first time!*

Available in Paperback and Kindle format from Amazon.

WRITE FAST, BEAT PROCRASTINATION
MILE-HIGH
WORD
COUNT
& WRITING PRODUCTIVITY
HOW TO CRUNCH 5000 WORDS
A DAY, EVERY DAY
Rick Smith
CreateSpace & Kindle Self-Publishing Masterclass

Write Fast, Write More, Beat Procrastination and Finish Your Book.

Nobody can buy your book until you finish writing it. Nothing happens until you publish. If you're struggling to get it done, maybe you need a System!

Perhaps you're already an Author, but you need a competitive edge. You need to write more books, and that takes time. Whatever the case, maybe you're holding yourself back:

- Do you struggle with procrastination and getting started each day?

- Are you easily distracted from your writing?

- With all your other responsibilities, is finding enough time to write a problem for you?

In 'Mile-High Word-Count', the latest Self-Publishing Masterclass from Bestselling Author Rick Smith, you'll discover proven systems and techniques that will supercharge your writing productivity:

- Secrets of the Five Hour Author: Write a new book every month in only 5 Hours a Week.

- The HITs Writing System: High-Intensity Interval Training for ambitious Authors.

- The Lean-Mean 5:2 Author: Write like a whirlwind for just 45 minutes a day: and take the Weekends off!

- The Mile-High Word-Count: 5000+ Words a day in only Four Weeks!

You'll also learn the *Secret Weapons* that will double or treble your Productivity when you're writing a book.

- 14 Top Tips to Beat Procrastination.

- 5 Simple Kick-Start methods that will make you Want To Write every day.

- Where to find amazing FREE Software that makes planning and organizing easy.

You could spend months or years trying to write faster, or you could learn all you need to know in a weekend in *"Mile High Word-Count"*. The book business is booming, but it's also highly competitive. Join the Winners; Leave Nothing to Chance.

Available in Paperback and Kindle format from Amazon.

Made in the USA
Middletown, DE
27 December 2016